EASY PESTO COOKBOOK

50 DELICIOUS PESTO RECIPES

By
Chef Maggie Chow
Copyright © 2015 by Saxonberg Associates
All rights reserved

Published by
BookSumo, a division of Saxonberg Associates
http://www.booksumo.com/

INTRODUCTION

Welcome to *The Effortless Chef Series*! Thank you for taking the time to download the *Easy Pesto Cookbook*. Come take a journey with me into the delights of easy cooking. The point of this cookbook and all my cookbooks is to exemplify the effortless nature of cooking simply.

In this book we focus on Pesto. You will find that even though the recipes are simple, the taste of the dishes is quite amazing.

So will you join me in an adventure of simple cooking? If the answer is yes (and I hope it is) please consult the table of contents to find the dishes you are most interested in. Once you are ready jump right in and start cooking.

— Chef Maggie Chow

TABLE OF CONTENTS

Introduction 2
Table of Contents 3
Any Issues? Contact Me 7
Legal Notes 8
Common Abbreviations 9
Chapter 1: Easy Pesto Recipes 10
    Classical Basil Chicken 10
    Basil and Olive Pizza 12
    South of the Border Pesto Sauce 14
    Arugula & Basil 16
    Simple Pesto 18
    Cheesy Artichoke Pesto 20
    American Pesto 22
    Pasta Pesto 24

Asian Peanut Pesto 26

Pesto Spirals 28

Spicy Pesto 30

Mushroom Pesto 32

Creamy Lettuce Pesto 35

Nutty Pesto 37

Pesto For Breakfast 39

Steamed Broccoli Pesto 41

Fresh Summer Pesto 43

Creamy & Cheesy Pesto Shrimp with Pasta 45

Cheesy Spinach Pesto 47

American Provolone Pesto 49

Cheesy Pesto Chicken & Pasta Bake 51

Baked Cheese Stuffed Pesto Meatballs 54

Pasta with Pesto Chicken & Spinach 57

Pasta with Cheesy Pesto Shrimp & Mushrooms 60

Parmesan Pesto 63

Brazilian Pesto 65

Cheesy Pesto Open-Faced 67

Classic Pesto 69

Cheesy Pro Quiche 71

Mozzarella Pesto Salad 73

Pesto Walnut Pasta 75

Pesto Lasagna 78

Pasta with Pesto Veggies 81

Swiss Pesto 84

French Pesto 86

Cheesy Pesto Omelet 88

Broiled Eggplant 90

Zucchini with Pesto & Cheese 93

Pesto Earth Apples 95

Mixed Medley Pesto 97

Macaroni in Creamy Beef Sauce 99

Pesto Steak 101

Pesto Pork 104

Creamy Pesto Olives 107

Fragrant Pesto 109

South East Asian Pesto From Vietnam 111

Cashew Pesto 114

Pesto Pink Pilaf 116

Pesto Fish 119

THANKS FOR READING! NOW LET'S TRY SOME **SUSHI** AND **DUMP DINNERS**.... 122

Come On 124

Let's Be Friends :) 124

Can I Ask A Favour? 125

Interested in Other Easy Cookbooks? 126

Any Issues? Contact Me

If you find that something important to you is missing from this book please contact me at maggie@booksumo.com.

I will try my best to re-publish a revised copy taking your feedback into consideration and let you know when the book has been revised with you in mind.

:)

— Chef Maggie Chow

Legal Notes

ALL RIGHTS RESERVED. NO PART OF THIS BOOK MAY BE REPRODUCED OR TRANSMITTED IN ANY FORM OR BY ANY MEANS. PHOTOCOPYING, POSTING ONLINE, AND / OR DIGITAL COPYING IS STRICTLY PROHIBITED UNLESS WRITTEN PERMISSION IS GRANTED BY THE BOOK'S PUBLISHING COMPANY. LIMITED USE OF THE BOOK'S TEXT IS PERMITTED FOR USE IN REVIEWS WRITTEN FOR THE PUBLIC AND/OR PUBLIC DOMAIN.

COMMON ABBREVIATIONS

cup(s)	C.
tablespoon	tbsp
teaspoon	tsp
ounce	oz.
pound	lb

*All units used are standard American measurements

Chapter 1: Easy Pesto Recipes

Classical Basil Chicken

Ingredients

- 4 skinless, boneless chicken breast halves
- 1/2 C. prepared basil pesto, divided
- 4 thin slices prosciutto, or more if needed

Directions

- Coat a baking dish with oil then set your oven to 400 degrees before doing anything else.
- Top each piece of chicken with 2 tbsps of pesto then cover each one with a piece of prosciutto.
- Then lay everything into the dish.
- Cook everything in the oven for 30 mins until the chicken is fully done.
- Enjoy.

Amount per serving (4 total)

Timing Information:

Preparation	10 m
Cooking	25 m
Total Time	35 m

Nutritional Information:

Calories	312 kcal
Fat	19.3 g
Carbohydrates	2g
Protein	31.5 g
Cholesterol	83 mg
Sodium	434 mg

* Percent Daily Values are based on a 2,000 calorie diet.

Basil and Olive Pizza

Ingredients

- 1 (12 inch) pre-baked pizza crust
- 1/2 C. pesto
- 1 ripe tomato, chopped
- 1/2 C. green bell pepper, chopped
- 1 (2 oz.) can chopped black olives, drained
- 1/2 small red onion, chopped
- 1 (4 oz.) can artichoke hearts, drained and sliced
- 1 C. crumbled feta cheese

Directions

- Set your oven to 450 degrees before doing anything else.
- Coat your pizza crust with the pesto sauce then layer the following on the crust: feta, tomatoes, artichokes, bell peppers, red onions, and olives.
- Cook the pizza in the oven for 12 mins.
- Enjoy.

Amount per serving (6 total)

Timing Information:

Preparation	10 m
Cooking	10 m
Total Time	20 m

Nutritional Information:

Calories	394 kcal
Fat	19.9 g
Carbohydrates	39.3g
Protein	17.3 g
Cholesterol	36 mg
Sodium	937 mg

* Percent Daily Values are based on a 2,000 calorie diet.

South of the Border Pesto Sauce

Ingredients

- 1/4 C. hulled pumpkin seeds (pepitas)
- 1 bunch cilantro
- 1/4 C. grated cotija cheese
- 4 cloves garlic
- 1 serrano chile pepper, seeded
- 1/2 tsp salt
- 6 tbsps olive oil

Directions

- Add the pumpkin seeds to the bowl of a food processor and chop everything with some pulses then combine in the olive oil, cilantro, salt, cheese, chile pepper, and garlic.
- Puree the mix then serve the pesto.
- Enjoy.

Amount per serving (6 total)

Timing Information:

Preparation	
Cooking	10 m
Total Time	10 m

Nutritional Information:

Calories	176 kcal
Fat	17.8 g
Carbohydrates	2.4g
Protein	2.9 g
Cholesterol	6 mg
Sodium	262 mg

* Percent Daily Values are based on a 2,000 calorie diet.

Arugula & Basil

Ingredients

- 1 1/2 C. baby arugula leaves
- 1 1/2 C. fresh basil leaves
- 2/3 C. pine nuts
- 8 cloves garlic
- 1 (6 oz.) can black olives, drained
- 3/4 C. extra virgin olive oil
- 1/2 lime, juiced
- 1 tsp red wine vinegar
- 1/8 tsp ground cumin
- 1 pinch ground cayenne pepper
- salt and pepper to taste

Directions

- In a large high-speed food processor, add the arugula, basil, olives, garlic and pine nuts and pulse till well combined.
- Add remaining ingredients and pulse till well combined and smooth.

Amount per serving (12 total)

Timing Information:

Preparation	
Cooking	15 m
Total Time	15 m

Nutritional Information:

Calories	191 kcal
Fat	19.4 g
Carbohydrates	3.2g
Protein	2.3 g
Cholesterol	0 mg
Sodium	125 mg

* Percent Daily Values are based on a 2,000 calorie diet.

Simple Pesto

Ingredients

- 1/4 C. almonds
- 3 cloves garlic
- 1 1/2 C. fresh basil leaves
- 1/2 C. olive oil
- 1 pinch ground nutmeg
- salt and pepper to taste

Directions

- Set your oven to 450 degrees F before doing anything else.
- Arrange the almonds onto a cookie sheet and bake for about 10 minutes or till toasted slightly.
- In a food processor, add the toasted almonds and the remaining ingredients till a rough paste forms.

Amount per serving (6 total)

Timing Information:

Preparation	2 m
Cooking	10 m
Total Time	12 m

Nutritional Information:

Calories	199 kcal
Fat	21.1 g
Carbohydrates	2g
Protein	1.7 g
Cholesterol	0 mg
Sodium	389 mg

* Percent Daily Values are based on a 2,000 calorie diet.

Cheesy Artichoke Pesto

Ingredients

- 2 C. fresh basil leaves
- 2 tbsps crumbled feta cheese
- 1/4 C. freshly grated Parmesan cheese
- 1/4 C. pine nuts, toasted
- 1 artichoke heart, roughly chopped
- 2 tbsps chopped oil-packed sun-dried tomatoes
- 1/2 C. extra-virgin olive oil
- 1 pinch salt and black pepper to taste

Directions

- In a large food processor, add all the ingredients except the oil and seasoning and pulse till combined.
- While the motor is running slowly, add the oil and pulse till smooth.
- Season with salt and black pepper and serve.

Amount per serving (12 total)

Timing Information:

Preparation	
Cooking	5 m
Total Time	5 m

Nutritional Information:

Calories	118 kcal
Fat	11.9 g
Carbohydrates	1.1g
Protein	2 g
Cholesterol	3 mg
Sodium	92 mg

* Percent Daily Values are based on a 2,000 calorie diet.

AMERICAN PESTO

Ingredients

- 4 C. packed fresh basil leaves
- 1/4 C. Italian parsley
- 2 cloves garlic, peeled and lightly crushed
- 1 C. pine nuts
- 1 1/2 C. shredded Parmigiano-Reggiano cheese
- 1 tbsp fresh lemon juice
- 1/2 C. extra-virgin olive oil, or more as needed
- salt and ground black pepper to taste

Directions

- In a food processor, add the parsley, basil, and garlic and pulse till chopped finely.
- Add the pine nuts and pulse till copped very finely as well.
- Add the cheese and pulse till combined.
- While the motor is running, slowly mix in the lemon juice.
- Then add the oil and pulse till well combined and smooth.
- Season with salt and black pepper and serve.

Amount per serving (6 total)

Timing Information:

Preparation	
Cooking	15 m
Total Time	15 m

Nutritional Information:

Calories	389 kcal
Fat	35.8 g
Carbohydrates	5.4g
Protein	14.1 g
Cholesterol	14 mg
Sodium	343 mg

* Percent Daily Values are based on a 2,000 calorie diet.

Pasta Pesto

Ingredients

- 4 C. fresh baby spinach
- 1/2 C. pecans
- 2 cloves garlic
- 1 C. Parmesan cheese
- 1 tbsp lemon juice
- 1/2 C. extra virgin olive oil
- 1 pinch salt and freshly ground black pepper to taste

Directions

- In a large food processor, add all the ingredients except the oil and pulse till combined.
- While the motor is running slowly, add the oil and pulse till well combined and smooth.

Amount per serving (16 total)

Timing Information:

Preparation	
Cooking	10 m
Total Time	10 m

Nutritional Information:

Calories	113 kcal
Fat	11.1 g
Carbohydrates	1.2g
Protein	2.5 g
Cholesterol	4 mg
Sodium	82 mg

* Percent Daily Values are based on a 2,000 calorie diet.

Easy Pesto Cookbook

Asian Peanut Pesto

Ingredients

- 1 bunch cilantro
- 1/4 C. peanut butter
- 3 cloves garlic, diced
- 3 tbsps extra-virgin olive oil
- 2 tbsps diced fresh ginger
- 1 1/2 tbsps fish sauce
- 1 tbsp brown sugar
- 1/2 tsp cayenne pepper

Directions

- In a blender or food processor, add all the ingredients and pulse till smooth.

Amount per serving (10 total)

Timing Information:

Preparation	
Cooking	10 m
Total Time	10 m

Nutritional Information:

Calories	84 kcal
Fat	7.4 g
Carbohydrates	3.4g
Protein	1.9 g
Cholesterol	0 mg
Sodium	197 mg

* Percent Daily Values are based on a 2,000 calorie diet.

Pesto Spirals

Ingredients

- 1 tbsp olive oil
- 4 small zucchini, cut into noodle-shape strands
- 1/2 C. drained and rinsed canned garbanzo beans (chickpeas)
- 3 tbsps pesto, or to taste
- salt and ground black pepper to taste
- 2 tbsps shredded white Cheddar cheese, or to taste

Directions

- In a skillet, heat oil on medium heat.
- Stir in the zucchini and cook for about 5-10 minutes or till all the liquid is absorbed.
- Stir in the pesto and chickpeas and immediately reduce the heat to medium-low and cook for about 5 minutes or till the chickpeas and zucchini noodles are coated completely.
- Stir in the salt and black pepper and immediately place the zucchini mixture onto serving plates.
- Garnish the dish with the cheese and serve immediately.

Amount per serving (2 total)

Timing Information:

Preparation	10 m
Cooking	10 m
Total Time	20 m

Nutritional Information:

Calories	319 kcal
Fat	21.3 g
Carbohydrates	23.1g
Protein	12.1 g
Cholesterol	16 mg
Sodium	511 mg

* Percent Daily Values are based on a 2,000 calorie diet.

SPICY PESTO

Ingredients

- 1/4 C. walnuts
- 2 cloves garlic
- 2 C. packed fresh basil leaves
- 3/4 C. shredded Parmagiano-Reggiano cheese
- 1 jalapeno pepper, stem removed
- 2/3 C. olive oil
- salt and ground black pepper to taste

Directions

- In a food processor, add the garlic and walnuts and pulse till chopped finely.
- Add the jalapeno, basil and cheese and pulse till well combined.
- While the motor is running slowly, add the oil and pulse till well combined and smooth.
- Season with salt and black pepper and serve.

Amount per serving (14 total)

Timing Information:

Preparation	
Cooking	10 m
Total Time	10 m

Nutritional Information:

Calories	126 kcal
Fat	13 g
Carbohydrates	0.8g
Protein	2.2 g
Cholesterol	4 mg
Sodium	66 mg

* Percent Daily Values are based on a 2,000 calorie diet.

Mushroom Pesto

Ingredients

- 2 tbsps butter
- 1 lb mixed fresh mushrooms (such as cremini, button, oyster, and portobello), quartered
- 1 shallot, chopped
- 1 C. toasted pine nuts
- 1/4 C. extra-virgin olive oil
- 1/4 C. vegetable broth
- 3 cloves garlic, chopped
- 1 tbsp freshly squeezed lemon juice
- 1 tsp kosher salt
- 1/2 tsp freshly ground black pepper
- 1/2 C. Parmesan cheese, grated

Directions

- In a pan, melt the butter on medium heat.
- Stir in the shallots and mushrooms and cook for about 5-7 minutes or till the mushrooms become golden brown.
- Remove from heat and keep aside to cool for about 10 minutes.
- In a blender, add the cooked mushroom mixture and remaining ingredients except cheese and pulse till grounded finely.

- Transfer the mixture into a bowl and stir in the cheese before serving.

Amount per serving (6 total)

Timing Information:

Preparation	15 m
Cooking	15 m
Total Time	30 m

Nutritional Information:

Calories	302 kcal
Fat	26.9 g
Carbohydrates	8.4g
Protein	10.8 g
Cholesterol	16 mg
Sodium	474 mg

* Percent Daily Values are based on a 2,000 calorie diet.

CREAMY LETTUCE PESTO

Ingredients

- 1/2 clove garlic
- 1/3 C. walnuts
- 3 oz. watercress, rinsed and dried
- 1 C. freshly grated Parmesan cheese
- 2 tbsps mayonnaise

Directions

- In a food processor, add all the ingredients and pulse till a smooth paste forms.

Amount per serving (8 total)

Timing Information:

Preparation	
Cooking	10 m
Total Time	10 m

Nutritional Information:

Calories	113 kcal
Fat	9.6 g
Carbohydrates	1.5g
Protein	5.9 g
Cholesterol	12 mg
Sodium	215 mg

* Percent Daily Values are based on a 2,000 calorie diet.

Nutty Pesto

Ingredients

- 2 C. basil leaves
- 1/2 C. walnuts
- 1/4 C. olive oil
- 2 cloves garlic
- 1 tbsp lemon juice

Directions

- In a food processor, add all the ingredients and pulse till a smooth paste forms.

Amount per serving (2 total)

Timing Information:

Preparation	
Cooking	10 m
Total Time	10 m

Nutritional Information:

Calories	455 kcal
Fat	47.3 g
Carbohydrates	6.9g
Protein	6.1 g
Cholesterol	0 mg
Sodium	3 mg

* Percent Daily Values are based on a 2,000 calorie diet.

Pesto For Breakfast

Ingredients

- 3/4 C. baking mix
- 1/3 C. water, or as needed
- 1 (8 oz.) package Cheddar cheese, shredded
- 5 tsps prepared pesto

Directions

- Grease your griddle then heat it completely.
- In a large bowl, add all the ingredients and mix till well combined.
- Place about 1/4 C. of the mixture onto the heated griddle and cook everything for about 2-3 minutes per side or till golden brown.
- Repeat with the remaining mixture.

Amount per serving (4 total)

Timing Information:

Preparation	5 m
Cooking	15 m
Total Time	20 m

Nutritional Information:

Calories	350 kcal
Fat	24.9 g
Carbohydrates	15g
Protein	16.7 g
Cholesterol	61 mg
Sodium	681 mg

* Percent Daily Values are based on a 2,000 calorie diet.

Steamed Broccoli Pesto

Ingredients

- 2 C. chopped broccoli florets
- 2 C. chopped fresh basil
- 1/4 C. extra-virgin olive oil
- 1/4 C. shaved Parmesan cheese
- 1/4 C. pine nuts
- 6 cloves garlic, peeled
- 2 tbsps vegetable broth, or more if needed
- 1 pinch cayenne pepper
- salt and ground black pepper to taste

Directions

- Arrange a steamer basket over a pan of water and bring to a boil on medium heat.
- Place broccoli into a steamer basket and cook, covered for about 3-5 minutes or till tender.
- Drain the broccoli well and transfer everything into a food processor with remaining ingredients and pulse till smooth.

Amount per serving (8 total)

Timing Information:

Preparation	15 m
Cooking	5 m
Total Time	20 m

Nutritional Information:

Calories	112 kcal
Fat	10 g
Carbohydrates	3.3g
Protein	3.1 g
Cholesterol	2 mg
Sodium	54 mg

* Percent Daily Values are based on a 2,000 calorie diet.

Fresh Summer Pesto

Ingredients

- 2 C. dandelion greens
- 1/2 C. olive oil
- 1/2 C. grated Parmesan cheese
- 2 tsps crushed garlic
- salt to taste (optional)
- 1 pinch red pepper flakes, or to taste (optional)

Directions

- In a food processor, add all the ingredients and pulse till smooth.

Amount per serving (16 total)

Timing Information:

Preparation	
Cooking	10 m
Total Time	10 m

Nutritional Information:

Calories	74 kcal
Fat	7.5 g
Carbohydrates	0.9g
Protein	1.2 g
Cholesterol	2 mg
Sodium	44 mg

* Percent Daily Values are based on a 2,000 calorie diet.

Creamy & Cheesy Pesto Shrimp with Pasta

Ingredients

- 1 lb linguine pasta
- 1/2 C. butter
- 2 C. heavy cream
- 1/2 tsp ground black pepper
- 1 C. grated Parmesan cheese
- 1/3 C. pesto
- 1 lb large shrimp, peeled and deveined

Directions

- In a large pan of lightly salted boiling water, add the pasta and cook for about 8-10 minutes or till desired doneness and drain well and keep aside. Meanwhile, melt the butter in a large skillet on medium heat. Add the cream and black pepper and cook, stirring continuously for about 6-8 minutes. Add the cheese and stir till well combined. Stir in the pesto and cook, stirring continuously for about 3-5 minutes. Add the shrimp and cook for about 3-5 minutes. Serve hot with pasta.

Amount per serving (8 total)

Timing Information:

Preparation	15 m
Cooking	15 m
Total Time	30 m

Nutritional Information:

Calories	646 kcal
Fat	42.5 g
Carbohydrates	43g
Protein	23.1 g
Cholesterol	210 mg
Sodium	437 mg

* Percent Daily Values are based on a 2,000 calorie diet.

Cheesy Spinach Pesto

Ingredients

- 1 1/2 C. baby spinach leaves
- 3/4 C. fresh basil leaves
- 1/2 C. toasted pine nuts
- 1/2 C. grated Parmesan cheese
- 4 cloves garlic, peeled and quartered
- 3/4 tsp kosher salt
- 1/2 tsp freshly ground black pepper
- 1 tbsp fresh lemon juice
- 1/2 tsp lemon zest
- 1/2 C. extra-virgin olive oil

Directions

- In a food processor, add 2 tbsps of oil and remaining ingredients and pulse till well combined.
- While the motor is running slowly, add the remaining oil and pulse till smooth.

Amount per serving (24 total)

Timing Information:

Preparation	
Cooking	20 m
Total Time	20 m

Nutritional Information:

Calories	67 kcal
Fat	6.6 g
Carbohydrates	0.8g
Protein	1.5 g
Cholesterol	1 mg
Sodium	87 mg

* Percent Daily Values are based on a 2,000 calorie diet.

American Provolone Pesto

Ingredients

- 2 slices Italian bread
- 1 tbsp softened butter, divided
- 1 tbsp prepared pesto sauce, divided
- 1 slice provolone cheese
- 2 slices tomato
- 1 slice American cheese

Directions

- Spread 1/2 tbsp of butter over 1 slice evenly. In a nonstick skillet, arrange the slice, buttered side down on medium heat.
- Place 1/2 tbsp of pesto on the top of buttered slice evenly, followed by a provolone cheese slice, tomato slices and American cheese slice.
- Place the remaining pesto over another slice evenly and cover the slice in the skillet, pesto side down.
- Now, spread the remaining butter on top of the sandwich and cook everything for about 5 minutes from both sides or till golden brown.

Amount per serving (1 total)

Timing Information:

Preparation	5 m
Cooking	10 m
Total Time	15 m

Nutritional Information:

Calories	503 kcal
Fat	36.5 g
Carbohydrates	24.2g
Protein	20.4 g
Cholesterol	82 mg
Sodium	1108 mg

* Percent Daily Values are based on a 2,000 calorie diet.

Cheesy Pesto Chicken & Pasta Bake

Ingredients

- 1/2 C. seasoned bread crumbs
- 1/2 C. grated Parmesan cheese
- 1 tbsp olive oil
- 1 (16 oz.) box penne pasta
- 6 C. cubed cooked chicken
- 4 C. shredded Italian cheese blend
- 3 C. fresh baby spinach
- 1 (15 oz.) can crushed tomatoes
- 1 (15 oz.) jar Alfredo sauce
- 1 (15 oz.) jar pesto sauce
- 1 1/2 C. milk

Directions

- Set your oven to 350 degrees F before doing anything else and coat a 13x9-inch baking dish with cooking spray.
- In a small bowl, add the Parmesan cheese, breadcrumbs and oil and mix till well combined and keep aside.
- In a large pan of lightly salted boiling water, add the pasta and cook for about 10-11 minutes or till desired doneness and drain well and keep aside.

- In the same time in a large bowl, add the remaining ingredients and mix then stir in the pasta.
- Lay the chicken mixture onto the prepared baking dish evenly and spread the Parmesan mixture on top evenly.
- Cook the dish in the oven for 40-45 minutes or till the top becomes golden brown and bubbly.

Amount per serving (12 total)

Timing Information:

Preparation	15 m
Cooking	1 h
Total Time	1 h 15 m

Nutritional Information:

Calories	760 kcal
Fat	47.2 g
Carbohydrates	40.7g
Protein	45.4 g
Cholesterol	114 mg
Sodium	1210 mg

* Percent Daily Values are based on a 2,000 calorie diet.

Baked Cheese Stuffed Pesto Meatballs

Ingredients

- 3 lbs ground turkey
- 1 C. finely chopped onion
- 4 garlic cloves, diced
- 1 egg
- 1 C. Italian-style bread crumbs
- 1/2 C. grated Parmigiano-Reggiano cheese
- 1/2 C. chopped fresh flat-leaf parsley
- 1/4 C. prepared pesto
- 1/4 C. milk
- 1 tbsp salt
- 2 tsps fresh ground black pepper
- 1 lb fresh mozzarella, cut into small cubes
- 3 tbsps extra-virgin olive oil
- 2 (24 oz.) jars marinara sauce

Directions

- Set your oven to 375 degrees F before doing anything else.
- In a large bowl, add the turkey, egg, Parmigiano-Reggiano cheese, pesto, milk, breadcrumbs, onion, garlic, parsley, salt and black pepper and mix till well combined and make 1 inch meatballs.

- With your fingers, create a hole in the center of each ball and, fill the holes with mozzarella cubes.
- In a nonstick skillet, arrange the meatballs in a single layer and drizzle with oil evenly.
- Cook the meatballs in the oven for 30 minutes or till the desired doneness.
- In a pan, add the marinara sauce on low heat and bring to a gentle simmer.
- Carefully, lay the meatballs in pan of marinara sauce and let them cook for at least 2 minutes.

Amount per serving (12 total)

Timing Information:

Preparation	35 m
Cooking	35 m
Total Time	1 h 10 m

Nutritional Information:

Calories	486 kcal
Fat	25.3 g
Carbohydrates	26g
Protein	38.3 g
Cholesterol	130 mg
Sodium	1621 mg

* Percent Daily Values are based on a 2,000 calorie diet.

Pasta with Pesto Chicken & Spinach

Ingredients

- 2 tbsps olive oil
- 2 cloves garlic, finely chopped
- 4 skinless, boneless chicken breast halves - cut into strips
- 2 C. fresh spinach leaves
- 1 (4.5 oz.) package dry Alfredo sauce mix
- 2 tbsps pesto
- 1 (8 oz.) package dry penne pasta
- 1 tbsp grated Romano cheese

Directions

- In a large skillet, heat oil on medium-high heat and sauté garlic for about 1 minute.
- Add the chicken and cook for about 7-8 minutes from both sides and stir in the spinach and cook for about 3-4 minutes.
- At the same time, prepare the Alfredo sauce according to the package's directions and add the pesto and stir to combine and keep aside.

- In a large pan of lightly salted boiling water, add the pasta and cook for about 8-10 minutes or till desired doneness and drain well.
- In a large bowl, add the cooked pasta, chicken mixture and pesto mixture and toss to coat well.
- Serve immediately with a garnishing of cheese.

Amount per serving (4 total)

Timing Information:

Preparation	20 m
Cooking	35 m
Total Time	55 m

Nutritional Information:

Calories	572 kcal
Fat	19.3 g
Carbohydrates	57.3g
Protein	41.9 g
Cholesterol	84 mg
Sodium	1707 mg

* Percent Daily Values are based on a 2,000 calorie diet.

Pasta with Cheesy Pesto Shrimp & Mushrooms

Ingredients

- 1 (16 oz.) package linguine pasta
- 2 tbsps olive oil
- 1 small onion, chopped
- 8 cloves garlic, sliced
- 1/2 C. butter
- 2 tbsps all-purpose flour
- 2 C. milk
- 1 pinch salt
- 1 pinch pepper
- 1 1/2 C. grated Romano cheese
- 1 C. prepared basil pesto
- 1 lb cooked shrimp, peeled and deveined
- 20 mushrooms, chopped
- 3 roma (plum) tomato, diced

Directions

- In a large pan of lightly salted boiling water, add the pasta and cook for about 8-10 minutes or till desired doneness and drain well and keep aside.

- In a large skillet, heat oil on medium heat and sauté the onion for about 4-5 minutes.
- Add the butter and garlic and sauté for about 1 minute.
- Meanwhile in a bowl, mix together milk and flour and pour into a skillet, stirring continuously.
- Stir in the salt and black pepper and cook, stirring for about 4 minutes.
- Add the cheese, stirring continuously till melted completely.
- Stir in the pesto and shrimp, tomatoes and mushrooms and cook for about 4 minutes or till heated completely.
- Add the pasta and toss to coat and serve immediately.

Amount per serving (8 total)

Timing Information:

Preparation	30 m
Cooking	20 m
Total Time	50 m

Nutritional Information:

Calories	677 kcal
Fat	38.3 g
Carbohydrates	52.2g
Protein	33.6 g
Cholesterol	155 mg
Sodium	719 mg

* Percent Daily Values are based on a 2,000 calorie diet.

Parmesan Pesto

Ingredients

- 1 (16 oz.) package penne pasta
- 2 tbsps butter
- 2 tbsps olive oil
- 4 skinless, boneless chicken breast halves - cut into thin strips
- 2 cloves garlic, diced
- salt and pepper to taste
- 1 1/4 C. heavy cream
- 1/4 C. pesto
- 3 tbsps grated Parmesan cheese

Directions

- In a large pan of lightly salted boiling water, add the pasta and cook for about 8-10 minutes or till desired doneness and drain well and keep aside.
- In a large skillet, heat oil and butter on medium heat and cook the chicken for about 5-6 minutes or till almost done.
- Reduce the heat to medium-low and stir in the remaining ingredients and cook till the chicken is done completely.
- Add the pasta and toss to coat well and serve immediately.

Amount per serving (8 total)

Timing Information:

Preparation	20 m
Cooking	10 m
Total Time	30 m

Nutritional Information:

Calories	497 kcal
Fat	26.1 g
Carbohydrates	42.6g
Protein	24 g
Cholesterol	97 mg
Sodium	164 mg

* Percent Daily Values are based on a 2,000 calorie diet.

Brazilian Pesto

Ingredients

- 3 C. chopped fresh basil
- 1 C. extra virgin olive oil
- 1/2 C. pine nuts
- 1/8 C. Brazil nuts
- 2/3 C. grated Parmesan cheese
- 2 tbsps diced garlic
- 1/2 tsp chili powder

Directions

- In a food processor, add all the ingredients except oil and pulse till a thick paste forms.
- While the motor is running slowly, add the oil and pulse till smooth.

Amount per serving (12 total)

Timing Information:

Preparation	
Cooking	15 m
Total Time	15 m

Nutritional Information:

Calories	234 kcal
Fat	23.9 g
Carbohydrates	1.9g
Protein	3.7 g
Cholesterol	4 mg
Sodium	70 mg

* Percent Daily Values are based on a 2,000 calorie diet.

Cheesy Pesto Open-Faced

Ingredients

- 1 (1 lb) loaf French baguette
- 2/3 C. mayonnaise
- 1/3 C. basil pesto
- 2 cloves garlic, diced
- 1/2 C. freshly grated Parmesan cheese
- salt to taste

Directions

- Set your oven to broiler before doing anything else.
- On a cookie sheet, place the bread slices in a single layer and broil for about 5-6 minutes or till toasted lightly. Remove everything from the oven and immediately place on a plate, changing the side of the bread slice, toasted side down. Now, set your oven to 350 degrees F before continuing. In a small bowl, add the remaining ingredients and mix till well combined. Spread the pesto mixture over the untoasted side of each slice evenly and arrange onto a cookie sheet. Cook everything in the oven for about 6-8 minutes.
- Now, set the oven to broiler and broil the sandwich till the top becomes golden brown and bubbly.

Amount per serving (8 total)

Timing Information:

Preparation	6 m
Cooking	12 m
Total Time	18 m

Nutritional Information:

Calories	375 kcal
Fat	22.1 g
Carbohydrates	33.8g
Protein	11.2 g
Cholesterol	16 mg
Sodium	648 mg

* Percent Daily Values are based on a 2,000 calorie diet.

Classic Pesto

Ingredients

- 1/3 C. pine nuts
- 2/3 C. olive oil
- 5 cloves garlic
- 1/3 C. nutritional yeast
- 1 bunch fresh basil leaves
- salt and pepper to taste

Directions

- In a heated nonstick skillet, add the pine nuts on medium heat and cook, stirring continuously till toasted.
- In a food processor, add the toasted pine nuts and remaining ingredients and pulse till smooth.

Amount per serving (16 total)

Timing Information:

Preparation	
Cooking	15 m
Total Time	15 m

Nutritional Information:

Calories	106 kcal
Fat	10.6 g
Carbohydrates	1.7g
Protein	2.2 g
Cholesterol	0 mg
Sodium	1 mg

* Percent Daily Values are based on a 2,000 calorie diet.

Cheesy Pro Quiche

Ingredients

- 4 tbsps pesto
- 1 (9 inch) unbaked pie crust
- 4 tbsps crumbled goat cheese
- 3 eggs
- 1/2 C. half-and-half cream
- 1 tbsp all-purpose flour
- 8 oil-packed sun-dried tomatoes, drained and cut into strips
- salt and freshly ground black pepper to taste

Directions

- Set your oven to 400 degrees F before doing anything else.
- In the bottom of a pie dish, place the pesto evenly and sprinkle with goat cheese.
- In a large bowl, add half-and-half, eggs, flour, salt and black pepper and beat till well combined.
- Place the egg mixture over the goat cheese evenly, followed by the sun-dried tomatoes.
- Cook everything in the oven for about 30 minutes.

Amount per serving (8 total)

Timing Information:

Preparation	15 m
Cooking	30 m
Total Time	45 m

Nutritional Information:

Calories	222 kcal
Fat	16.1 g
Carbohydrates	13.1g
Protein	6.6 g
Cholesterol	81 mg
Sodium	235 mg

* Percent Daily Values are based on a 2,000 calorie diet.

Mozzarella Pesto Salad

Ingredients

- 1 1/2 C. rotini pasta
- 3 tbsps pesto, or to taste
- 1 tbsp extra-virgin olive oil
- 1/4 tsp salt, or to taste
- 1/4 tsp granulated garlic
- 1/8 tsp ground black pepper
- 1/2 C. halved grape tomatoes
- 1/2 C. small (pearlini) fresh mozzarella balls
- 2 leaves fresh basil leaves, finely shredded

Directions

- In a large pan of lightly salted boiling water, add the pasta and cook for about 8 minutes or till desired doneness and drain well and keep aside.
- In a large bowl, mix together pesto, granulated garlic, oil, salt and black pepper and add the pasta and toss to coat.
- Gently, fold in the mozzarella, tomatoes and basil and serve immediately.

Amount per serving (6 total)

Timing Information:

Preparation	10 m
Cooking	10 m
Total Time	20 m

Nutritional Information:

Calories	169 kcal
Fat	8.3 g
Carbohydrates	17.1g
Protein	6.1 g
Cholesterol	10 mg
Sodium	173 mg

* Percent Daily Values are based on a 2,000 calorie diet.

Pesto Walnut Pasta

Ingredients

- olive oil
- 2 lbs fresh spinach, cleaned
- 2 lbs nonfat ricotta cheese
- 4 large cloves garlic, diced
- 1/2 tsp salt
- Freshly ground black pepper to taste
- 1/2 C. grated Parmesan cheese
- 1/3 C. diced walnuts, lightly toasted
- 1 (24 oz.) jar tomato sauce
- 16 fresh, uncooked lasagna noodles
- 1/2 lb mozzarella, grated

Walnut Pesto:

- 3 C. packed fresh basil leaves
- 3 large cloves garlic
- 1/3 C. lightly toasted walnuts
- 1/3 C. extra virgin olive oil
- 1/3 C. grated Parmesan cheese
- Salt and pepper to taste
- Additional extra-virgin olive oil (for storage)

Directions

- Set your oven to 350 degrees F before doing anything else and coat a 13x9-inch casserole dish with some cooking spray.
- For the pesto, in a food processor, add basil, garlic and walnuts and pulse till chopped finely.
- While the motor is running slowly, add the oil and pulse till smooth and transfer into a bowl and mix in the parmesan, salt and black pepper.
- In a large bowl, mix together the cottage or ricotta cheese, half of the parmesan, pesto, spinach, garlic, walnuts, salt and black pepper.
- Place half of the tomato sauce in the bottom of the prepared baking dish and place 1 layer of uncooked lasagna noodles over the tomato sauce.
- Place one-third of the spinach mixture over the noodles, followed by 1/3 of the mozzarella.
- Repeat the layers once, and finish up with the last layer of noodles.
- Cover and cook in the oven for about 35 minutes.
- Uncover the casserole dish and sprinkle the top of the lasagna with the reserved Parmesan cheese and cook for 15 minutes more.

Amount per serving (8 total)

Timing Information:

Preparation	30 m
Cooking	1 h
Total Time	1 h 30 m

Nutritional Information:

Calories	638 kcal
Fat	27.2 g
Carbohydrates	64.3g
Protein	32.6 g
Cholesterol	45 mg
Sodium	1025 mg

* Percent Daily Values are based on a 2,000 calorie diet.

Pesto Lasagna

Ingredients

- 1/4 C. pine nuts
- 3 C. fresh basil leaves
- 3/4 C. grated Parmesan cheese
- 1/2 C. olive oil
- 4 cloves garlic
- 12 lasagna noodles
- cooking spray
- 3 tbsps olive oil
- 1 C. chopped onion
- 3 cloves garlic, crushed
- 2 (12 oz.) packages frozen chopped spinach
- 3 C. diced cooked chicken breast
- 1 tsp salt
- 1 tsp ground black pepper
- 2 C. ricotta cheese
- 3/4 C. grated Parmesan cheese
- 1 egg
- 2 C. shredded mozzarella cheese

Directions

- Set your oven to 350 degrees F before doing anything else and coat a 13x9-inch casserole dish with some cooking spray.

- In a heated nonstick skillet, add the pine nuts on medium heat and cook, stirring often for about 3 minutes or till toasted.
- In a food processor, add the toasted pine nuts and the remaining pesto ingredients and pulse till smooth and keep aside.
- For the lasagna, in a large pan of lightly salted boiling water, add the lasagna noodles and cook them for about 8-10 minutes or till desired doneness and drain well and keep aside.
- In a large skillet, heat oil on medium-high heat and sauté the onion and garlic for about 5 minutes.
- Add the spinach and cook for about 5 minutes.
- Add the chicken and cook for about 5 minutes and stir in some salt and black pepper and remove from heat and let it cool.
- In a bowl, mix together parmesan, ricotta, egg, 1 1/2 C. of pesto and chicken mixture.
- Place the remaining pesto in the bottom of the prepared casserole dish evenly and top everything with 4 lasagna noodles.
- Place one-third of the chicken mixture over the noodles evenly and followed by one-third of the mozzarella and repeat the layers twice.
- Cook everything in the oven for about 35-40 minutes or till the top becomes golden brown and bubbly.

Amount per serving (8 total)

Timing Information:

Preparation	25 m
Cooking	1 h 6 m
Total Time	1 h 31 m

Nutritional Information:

Calories	675 kcal
Fat	38.4 g
Carbohydrates	38.3g
Protein	46.5 g
Cholesterol	118 mg
Sodium	887 mg

* Percent Daily Values are based on a 2,000 calorie diet.

Pasta with Pesto Veggies

Ingredients

- 1 C. fresh basil leaves
- 2 cloves garlic, diced
- 1/4 C. pine nuts
- 1/2 C. Parmesan cheese
- 1/4 C. olive oil
- 2 tbsps lemon juice
- 4 C. mini penne pasta
- 1 tbsp olive oil
- 1 tbsp olive oil
- 1/4 C. pine nuts
- 1 C. chopped asparagus
- 1/2 C. sliced zucchini
- 1/2 C. sliced Kalamata olives
- 1/2 C. diced roasted red pepper
- 1/2 C. chopped sun-dried tomatoes
- 1/2 C. grated Parmesan cheese

Directions

- In a large pan of lightly salted boiling water, add the pasta and cook for about 11 minutes or till desired doneness and drain well and transfer into a bowl with 1 tbsp of oil and keep aside.

- Meanwhile in a food processor, add basil, garlic, 1/2 C. of cheese, 1/4 C. of oil, 1/4 C. of pine nuts and lemon juice and pulse till smooth and keep aside.
- In a large skillet, heat the remaining oil on medium heat and cook the remaining 1/4 C. of pine nuts.
- Cook till golden brown and transfer onto a plate and keep aside.
- In the same skillet, add the remaining ingredients except the cheese and cook for about 5-7 minutes and stir in the pine nuts.
- Add the desired amount of pesto and pasta and toss to combine.
- Serve immediately with a garnishing of cheese.

Amount per serving (8 total)

Timing Information:

Preparation	20 m
Cooking	20 m
Total Time	40 m

Nutritional Information:

Calories	367 kcal
Fat	20.6 g
Carbohydrates	34.4g
Protein	12.6 g
Cholesterol	9 mg
Sodium	413 mg

* Percent Daily Values are based on a 2,000 calorie diet.

Swiss Pesto

Ingredients

- 1/2 C. olive oil, divided
- 10 leaves Swiss chard, chopped
- 4 cloves garlic, chopped
- 1 C. basil leaves
- 1 C. pecans
- 1/2 tsp sea salt
- 1 tbsp lemon juice
- 1 (3 oz.) package grated Parmesan cheese
- salt and ground black pepper to taste

Directions

- In a skillet, heat 2 tbsp f oil on medium heat and cook the garlic and Swiss chard for about 3-5 minutes and remove from heat and keep aside to cool.
- In a food processor, add the remaining oil, basil, cheese, pecans and sea salt and pulse till well combined.
- Add the lemon juice and cooked Swiss chard mixture and pulse till a smooth puree forms.
- Season with salt and black pepper and serve.

Amount per serving (10 total)

Timing Information:

Preparation	20 m
Cooking	5 m
Total Time	25 m

Nutritional Information:

Calories	228 kcal
Fat	22.1 g
Carbohydrates	4.4g
Protein	5.4 g
Cholesterol	7 mg
Sodium	319 mg

* Percent Daily Values are based on a 2,000 calorie diet.

French Pesto

Ingredients

- 1 (8 oz.) package goat cheese, softened
- 1 (8 oz.) jar pesto, or as needed
- 3 tomatoes, chopped
- 1 (8 oz.) loaf French bread, sliced

Directions

- In a large serving plate, slice the cheese into a 1/4-inch layer.
- Place the pesto over the cheese evenly in a thin layer, followed by the tomatoes.
- Enjoy this dip with the sliced French bread.

Amount per serving (12 total)

Timing Information:

Preparation	
Cooking	15 m
Total Time	15 m

Nutritional Information:

Calories	231 kcal
Fat	15.3 g
Carbohydrates	13.9g
Protein	10.3 g
Cholesterol	21 mg
Sodium	377 mg

* Percent Daily Values are based on a 2,000 calorie diet.

Cheesy Pesto Omelet

Ingredients

- 1 tsp olive oil
- 1 portobello mushroom cap, sliced
- 1/4 C. chopped red onion
- 4 egg whites
- 1 tsp water
- salt and ground black pepper to taste
- 1/4 C. shredded low-fat mozzarella cheese
- 1 tsp prepared pesto

Directions

- In a skillet, heat oil on medium heat and cook the onion and mushroom for about 3-5 minutes.
- In a small bowl, add water, egg whites, salt and black pepper and beat well.
- Add the egg whites mixture into the skillet and cook, stirring often, for about 5 minutes or till the egg whites begin to firm.
- Place the cheese over the omelet, followed by the pesto and carefully, fold the omelet and cook for about 2-3 minutes or till the cheese is melted.

Amount per serving (1 total)

Timing Information:

Preparation	10 m
Cooking	15 m
Total Time	25 m

Nutritional Information:

Calories	259 kcal
Fat	12 g
Carbohydrates	12g
Protein	28 g
Cholesterol	19 mg
Sodium	888 mg

* Percent Daily Values are based on a 2,000 calorie diet.

Broiled Eggplant

Ingredients

- 1/2 C. olive oil, for frying
- 2 large eggplants, halved lengthwise
- 1 pinch salt and ground black pepper to taste
- 1/4 C. fresh basil leaves
- 3 cloves garlic, diced
- 2 tbsps pine nuts
- 2 tbsps freshly grated Parmesan cheese
- 3 tbsps extra-virgin olive oil, for pesto

Directions

- Set your oven's broiler to low and arrange the rack about 6-inches from the heating element.
- With a sharp knife, cut slits in a crisscross design in each eggplant half (Be careful not to pierce the skin) and season the eggplant with salt and black pepper
- In a large skillet, heat 1/2 C. of olive oil on medium heat.

- Carefully, place the eggplant halves in the skillet, skin side facing upwards and cook for about 10 minutes or till golden brown.
- Change the side and cook for about 2-3 minutes and transfer onto a paper towel lined plate.
- Meanwhile in a food processor, add the basil, garlic, cheese, pine nuts and half of the oil and pulse till well combined.
- While the motor is running slowly, add the remaining oil and pulse till smooth.
- In a broiler pan, place the eggplant halves, skin side down and top each half with pesto.
- Broil for about 7-10 minutes or till the top becomes bubbly.

Amount per serving (2 total)

Timing Information:

Preparation	15 m
Cooking	20 m
Total Time	35 m

Nutritional Information:

Calories	663 kcal
Fat	54.4 g
Carbohydrates	41.9g
Protein	11.3 g
Cholesterol	4 mg
Sodium	92 mg

* Percent Daily Values are based on a 2,000 calorie diet.

Zucchini with Pesto & Cheese

Ingredients

- 4 zucchini, sliced
- 1 C. basil pesto
- 4 tbsps Parmesan cheese

Directions

- In a steamer, arrange the zucchini over about 1-inch of boiling water.
- Cook, covered for about 2-6 minutes or till the desired doneness is achieved.
- Transfer the zucchini into a serving bowl with the pesto and mix well.
- Serve with a garnishing of cheese.

Amount per serving (4 total)

Timing Information:

Preparation	10 m
Cooking	6 m
Total Time	16 m

Nutritional Information:

Calories	363 kcal
Fat	30.2 g
Carbohydrates	10.8g
Protein	15.5 g
Cholesterol	24 mg
Sodium	572 mg

* Percent Daily Values are based on a 2,000 calorie diet.

Pesto Earth Apples

Ingredients

- 10 small ripe tomatoes
- 1/2 C. homemade or purchased pesto
- 1 C. grated Parmesan cheese

Directions

- Set your oven to 350 degrees F before doing anything else and coat a baking dish with oil.
- Cut the tomatoes in half, lengthwise and discard about 1 tbsp of flesh from the center.
- Fill the tomato halves with pesto and top with the cheese evenly.
- Arrange the tomatoes into the prepared baking dish in a single layer, filling side upwards.
- Cook everything in the oven till the top becomes golden brown and bubbly.

Amount per serving (10 total)

Timing Information:

Preparation	15 m
Cooking	15 m
Total Time	30 m

Nutritional Information:

Calories	121 kcal
Fat	8.7 g
Carbohydrates	4.8g
Protein	6.9 g
Cholesterol	13 mg
Sodium	253 mg

* Percent Daily Values are based on a 2,000 calorie diet.

Mixed Medley Pesto

Ingredients

- 6 1/2 C. water
- 6 cubes vegetable broth
- 2 medium potatoes, cubed
- 2 carrots, diced
- 1 medium onion, diced
- 1 large zucchini, cubed
- 2 tbsps sun-dried tomato pesto

Directions

- In a large pan, add the water and bring to a boil on medium heat and dissolve the vegetable broth cubes completely.
- Add all the vegetables and cook for about 10 minutes and reduce the heat to low.
- Stir in the pesto and simmer for about 35 minutes or till the potatoes are done completely.

Amount per serving (4 total)

Timing Information:

Preparation	15 m
Cooking	45 m
Total Time	1 h

Nutritional Information:

Calories	134 kcal
Fat	1.7 g
Carbohydrates	27.5g
Protein	3.9 g
Cholesterol	0 mg
Sodium	60 mg

* Percent Daily Values are based on a 2,000 calorie diet.

Macaroni in Creamy Beef Sauce

Ingredients

- 1 (16 oz.) package elbow macaroni
- 1 lb ground beef
- 1/2 C. pesto
- 1/2 C. sour cream

Directions

- In a large pan of lightly salted boiling water, add the macaroni and cook for about 8-10 minutes or till desired doneness and drain well and keep aside.
- In a large skillet, heat oil on medium-high heat and cook beef for about 5-7 minutes or till browned and drain the all grease.
- Add the cream and pesto and stir to combine.
- Cook till warmed completely.
- Stir in the macaroni and serve immediately.

Amount per serving (6 total)

Timing Information:

Preparation	5 m
Cooking	15 m
Total Time	20 m

Nutritional Information:

Calories	581 kcal
Fat	26.4 g
Carbohydrates	57.9g
Protein	26.6 g
Cholesterol	62 mg
Sodium	217 mg

* Percent Daily Values are based on a 2,000 calorie diet.

Pesto Steak

Ingredients

- 4 cloves garlic
- 2 C. packed fresh basil leaves
- 1/3 C. pine nuts
- 1/2 C. extra-virgin olive oil
- 1/2 C. freshly grated Parmesan cheese
- 1 1/2 tbsps fresh lemon juice
- 3/4 tsp red pepper flakes
- 6 (6 oz.) flat iron steaks
- 2 large cloves garlic, diced
- salt and pepper to taste

Directions

- Set your grill to medium-high heat and coat the grill grate with a little cooking spray.
- In a food processor, add the basil, 4 garlic cloves, and pine nuts and pulse till chopped finely.

- While the motor is running slowly, add the oil and pulse till smooth.
- Add the lemon juice, cheese, red pepper flakes, salt and black pepper and pulse till well combined and smooth and keep aside.
- Rub the steak with the remaining 2 garlic cloves evenly and sprinkle with salt and black pepper.
- Cook the steak on the grill for about 4 minutes from both sides, coating with a little pesto mixture occasionally.
- Serve the steak with a topping of any remaining pesto.

Amount per serving (6 total)

Timing Information:

Preparation	20 m
Cooking	10 m
Total Time	30 m

Nutritional Information:

Calories	569 kcal
Fat	44.2 g
Carbohydrates	3.5g
Protein	40.1 g
Cholesterol	122 mg
Sodium	213 mg

* Percent Daily Values are based on a 2,000 calorie diet.

Pesto Pork

Ingredients

- 6 pork chops
- 1 tsp garlic powder
- 1 tsp seasoned salt, or to taste
- 2 eggs
- 1/4 C. all-purpose flour
- 2 C. Italian-style seasoned bread crumbs
- 1/4 C. olive oil
- 1 (10.75 oz.) can condensed cream of chicken soup
- 1/2 C. milk
- 3 tbsps pesto

Directions

- Set your oven to 350 degrees F before doing anything else.
- Sprinkle the chops with the seasoned salt and garlic powder.
- In a shallow dish, place the flour and beat eggs in a second shallow dish and place the breadcrumbs in a third shallow dish.
- First, roll the chops in flour evenly and shake off the excess flour.
- Now, dip the chops in the egg evenly and roll in breadcrumbs evenly.

- In a large skillet, heat oil on medium-high heat and cook the chops for about 5 minutes from both sides.
- Now, place the chops onto a baking dish in a single layer.
- With a large piece foil, cover the baking dish and cook it in oven for about 1 hour.
- Meanwhile in a bowl, add the remaining ingredients and beat till well combined.
- Uncover the baking sheet and place the pesto mixture over the chops evenly.
- Again, cover the baking dish with foil and cook everything in the oven for about 30 minutes more.

Amount per serving (6 total)

Timing Information:

Preparation	20 m
Cooking	1 h 40 m
Total Time	2 h

Nutritional Information:

Calories	531 kcal
Fat	26.6 g
Carbohydrates	36.5g
Protein	35.1 g
Cholesterol	129 mg
Sodium	1251 mg

* Percent Daily Values are based on a 2,000 calorie diet.

Creamy Pesto Olives

Ingredients

- 1 (6 oz.) can albacore tuna in water, drained and flaked
- 2 tbsps mayonnaise
- 1 tbsp basil pesto sauce
- 1 tsp lemon juice
- 1 pinch ground black pepper
- 1 (10 inch) flour tortilla
- 4 leaves lettuce
- 1 slice provolone cheese
- 5 pitted kalamata olives, cut in half

Directions

- In a bowl, add the tuna, pesto, mayonnaise, black pepper and lemon juice and gently, stir to combine.
- In a microwave safe plate, place the tortilla wrap and microwave on high for about 5-10 seconds or till just warmed.
- Place the tuna mixture onto the tortilla, followed by the olives, cheese and lettuce.
- Fold the tortilla bottom up about 2-inch to seal the filling and roll to form a wrap and serve.

Amount per serving (1 total)

Timing Information:

Preparation	
Cooking	15 m
Total Time	15 m

Nutritional Information:

Calories	870 kcal
Fat	52 g
Carbohydrates	42.3g
Protein	56.5 g
Cholesterol	1106 mg
Sodium	1912 mg

* Percent Daily Values are based on a 2,000 calorie diet.

Fragrant Pesto

Ingredients

- 1 lb garlic scapes, cut into 2-inch pieces
- 1 1/4 C. grated Parmesan cheese
- 1 C. olive oil
- 1 tbsp lemon juice
- ground black pepper to taste

Directions

- In a food processor, add all the ingredients and pulse till smooth.

Amount per serving (28 total)

Timing Information:

Preparation	
Cooking	10 m
Total Time	10 m

Nutritional Information:

Calories	108 kcal
Fat	8.8 g
Carbohydrates	5.6g
Protein	2.4 g
Cholesterol	3 mg
Sodium	58 mg

* Percent Daily Values are based on a 2,000 calorie diet.

South East Asian Pesto From Vietnam

Ingredients

- 1 lb dried rice noodles
- 1 1/2 C. chopped fresh cilantro
- 1/2 C. sweet Thai basil
- 2 cloves garlic, halved
- 1/2 tsp diced lemon grass bulb
- 1 jalapeno pepper, seeded and diced
- 1 tbsp vegetarian fish sauce
- 4 tbsps chopped, unsalted dry-roasted peanuts
- 7 tbsps canola oil
- 1/2 lime, cut into wedges
- salt and pepper to taste

Directions

- In a large bowl of cold water, soak the noodles for about 30 minutes and drain and keep aside.
- In a food processor, add the basil, cilantro, garlic, jalapeno, lemongrass, fish sauce and 2 tbsps of peanuts and pulse till chopped roughly.
- While the motor is running slowly, add the oil and pulse till smooth.

- Add remaining peanuts and pulse till the peanuts are chopped roughly.
- In a large skillet, add 1/2 C. of water and noodles on medium-high heat and cook for about 5 minutes or till most of the liquid is evaporated.
- Add the pesto and stir to combine well and serve immediately.

NOTE: You can season the pasta with more fish sauce, lime juice, salt and black pepper according to your taste

Amount per serving (4 total)

Timing Information:

Preparation	30 m
Cooking	5 m
Total Time	35 m

Nutritional Information:

Calories	694 kcal
Fat	29.8 g
Carbohydrates	98.8g
Protein	6.8 g
Cholesterol	0 mg
Sodium	217 mg

* Percent Daily Values are based on a 2,000 calorie diet.

Cashew Pesto

Ingredients

- 2 C. fresh cilantro leaves
- 1 C. fresh parsley leaves
- 3 tbsps lime juice
- 1 C. chili-lime cashews
- 1/2 C. olive oil
- 1 tsp salt
- 1 tsp black pepper
- 1 tsp cayenne pepper
- 1/2 C. grated Asiago cheese

Directions

- In a food processor, add all the ingredients and pulse till smooth. (You can add more oil if pesto is too thick)

Amount per serving (16 total)

Timing Information:

Preparation	
Cooking	15 m
Total Time	18 m

Nutritional Information:

Calories	125 kcal
Fat	11.8 g
Carbohydrates	3.6g
Protein	2.4 g
Cholesterol	3 mg
Sodium	246 mg

* Percent Daily Values are based on a 2,000 calorie diet.

PESTO PINK PILAF

Ingredients

- 1 1/2 lbs salmon fillets, cut into 1 inch cubes
- 1/3 C. pesto
- 2 tbsps butter
- 2 shallots, finely chopped
- 1 C. uncooked long-grain white rice
- 2 1/2 C. fish stock
- 2/3 C. dry white wine

Directions

- In a bowl, add salmon and pesto and toss to coat well and keep aside.
- Melt butter in a pan on medium heat and sauté the shallots for about 2-3 minutes or till tender.
- Add wine, broth and rice and stir to combine and bring to a boil.
- Reduce the heat to low and simmer, covered for about 15 minutes.

- Uncover the pan and place the salmon over rice and simmer, covered for about 25-30 minutes or till salmon and rice are done completely.

Amount per serving (4 total)

Timing Information:

Preparation	15 m
Cooking	45 m
Total Time	1 h

Nutritional Information:

Calories	710 kcal
Fat	34.9 g
Carbohydrates	44.2g
Protein	44.6 g
Cholesterol	122 mg
Sodium	778 mg

* Percent Daily Values are based on a 2,000 calorie diet.

Pesto Fish

Ingredients

- 1/4 C. pine nuts
- 1/2 C. coarsely chopped fresh basil
- 1/4 C. grated Parmesan cheese
- 1 clove garlic, diced
- 3 tbsps extra-virgin olive oil
- salt and freshly ground black pepper to taste
- 1 lb salmon fillet

Directions

- Set your grill for medium-high heat and coat the grill grate with a little cooking spray.
- Add pine nuts in a pre-heated small nonstick skillet on medium heat and cook, stirring for about 5 minutes or till toasted.
- In a food processor, add toasted pine nuts, Parmesan, basil and garlic and pulse till a thick paste forms.

- While the motor is running slowly, add the oil and pulse till smooth and season with salt and black pepper.
- Place the salmon fillets over the grill grate, skin side down and cook, covered for about 8-15 minutes or till salmon is about 2/3 done.
- Now, place the salmon fillets onto a baking sheet and cover each fillet with pesto evenly.
- Set your oven's broiler for heating and arrange the rack about 6 inches from the heating element.
- Broil the salmon fillets for about 5 minutes or till the salmon is done and the pesto becomes bubbly.

Amount per serving (4 total)

Timing Information:

Preparation	15 m
Cooking	20 m
Total Time	35 m

Nutritional Information:

Calories	354 kcal
Fat	25.6 g
Carbohydrates	1.8g
Protein	28.3 g
Cholesterol	81 mg
Sodium	174 mg

* Percent Daily Values are based on a 2,000 calorie diet.

Thanks for Reading! Now Let's Try some Sushi and Dump Dinners....

http://bit.ly/2443TFg

To grab this **box set** simply follow the link mentioned above, or tap the book cover.

This will take you to a page where you can simply enter your email address and a PDF version of the **box set** will be emailed to you.

I hope you are ready for some serious cooking!

http://bit.ly/2443TFg

You will also receive updates about all my new books when they are free.

Also don't forget to like and subscribe on the social networks. I love meeting my readers. Links to all my profiles are below so please click and connect :)

Facebook

Twitter

Come On...
Let's Be Friends :)

I adore my readers and love connecting with them socially. Please follow the links below so we can connect on Facebook, Twitter, and Google+.

Facebook

Twitter

I also have a blog that I regularly update for my readers so check it out below.

My Blog

Can I Ask A Favour?

If you found this book interesting, or have otherwise found any benefit in it. Then may I ask that you post a review of it on Amazon? Nothing excites me more than new reviews, especially reviews which suggest new topics for writing. I do read all reviews and I always factor feedback into my newer works.

So if you are willing to take ten minutes to write what you sincerely thought about this book then please visit our Amazon page and post your opinions.

Again thank you!

Interested in Other Easy Cookbooks?

Everything is easy! Check out my Amazon Author page for more great cookbooks:

For a complete listing of all my books please see my author pag.

Printed in Great Britain
by Amazon